How to A  e Intelligence of your Lagotto Romagnolo

A More Intelligent Lagotto Romagnolo is also a More Obedient Lagotto Romagnolo

Tina W. White

Table of Contents

Introduction

Greetings, my friend.

I am Tina W. White, and I'm writing here to talk about a topic which, sadly, is not very common: the intelligence of your Lagotto Romagnolo.

If you are reading this, it's possible that THIS is the root of any bad behavior of your Lagotto Romagnolo. Maybe it barks no matter what, it's aggressive, it pees everywhere or pulls the leash, just to give you a few examples.

Is it so smart that it chooses to ignore you? Does it know that what it does is wrong, and manipulate you? Or... is it so dumb that it does not understand? Well, the correct answer is... none.

It's so easy to believe in those ideas...

"Just look how he hides! He knows very well that he shouldn't have done it..." "Bad dog! Don't you see that peeing in the bedroom is just WRONG?" "Why doesn't she obey? She is so dummy!"

Half of the time, a dog's intelligence is doubted, and the other half, it's negative: or it is too dumb to obey, or too smart to obey.

Those thoughts are not yours... are from a society which never stopped to look a bit further. So, if Your Lagotto Romagnolo has a bad behavior, it's not its fault, nor it's yours. Bad habits don't come from a low intelligence, but from something really different.

Most of the time, to teach some rules and obedience to a dog we use basic training. It can work really well... or not at all. Sometimes we need to adapt a little bit, and prioritize something different: stimulus.

That's what I'm offering: through those pages, I'm going to show you different ways to stimulate the body, mind and senses of your Lagotto Romagnolo, which will improve its intelligence and capacity to understand, learn and memorize your instructions.

This is not the usual training guide: while I will write about a dog's needs and how to provide so you will get the best behavior, I'm not going to focus on psychology, but the methods to stimulate intelligence. That's why you are here.

I'm not offering a miracle. Reading this book will not make your Lagotto Romagnolo suddenly to be smarter and more obedient; to get that you will need to make an effort, you and it, so it won't work overnight.

What I DO offer is a series of methods, and you can use all of them or choose what is best suited for you. Thos methods will help to improve the intellect of your Lagotto Romagnolo, and, with a few training bases I'm going to teach you, will come in handy to teach orders, be obedient and make tricks you never thought would be possible.

So, do you want your Lagotto Romagnolo to be able to COUNT, or recognize very different objects? You can get it, with this.

Do you want it to obey your orders and never pee in the dining room again, chew your shoes or bark non-stop? Relax, that's what you are getting!

Some Preliminary Issues

First of all, I want to talk about a few things with you, like...

Do you know what is the medium level of intelligence in a dog? Do you really know where this intellect will drive a dog? Is it true that it can be improved? So, can it get WORSE?

Starting with some basics

Today, dogs are one of the most adaptable animals in nature, which points out to a certain degree of intelligence.

Although, this adaptability comes not only from intellect, but also instinct and even genetics.

I'm going to show you a very harsh example, but it explains very clearly the immense capacity of adaptation of every canine:

I'm sure you heard about coats or scarfs made with fox fur —fox is a canine—. However, it seems that every effort to preserve this valuable fur in captivity has failed: after just two or three generations, foxes evolve, lose the most flashy qualities of their fur because they don't need them anymore, and start to resemble more dogs than foxes.

That's just an example about how the canine genetics is predisposed to evolucion and fast change. And that's why we have so many different breeds.

So, in summary, to evolve and adapt these fast dogs need a good degree of intelligence.

If not, how on Earth would they be able to perform so many tasks, all what we asked from them from the very beginning? We needed dogs to protect the cattle, or the house, or to hunt, or to warn when there was a strange approaching... Now they detect bombs or drugs, they can even send messages.

In summary, dogs are always learning new tasks, new tricks, new games.
But, can every dog learn those things?
Well, yeah. Even a Chihuahua could learn to detect drugs, correctly trained, although it's always a good thing to take into account their own qualities: as a hunting dog, it's always better to be a Basset Hound than a Pug.

Intellectual limits in dogs

I want to show you a few pieces of information about canine intelligence, just so give you a general idea:

First and surprisingly, the intellect of a dog is equal to that of a three years old kid.
It means that with a well developed and stimulated intellect, a dog can learn around one hundred words.

They can also learn complex instructions, like...

- Bark three times
- Take the blue ball
- Which one is the racket?

Stimulating their mind and settling some training basics, a dog may remember and link around fifty different orders.

And those are only a few examples! My point is, dogs are much more smart than we may think, they can be compared with young humans and may learn many things... if and when we teach and stimulate them correctly.

Types of Canine Intelligence

It's very common to believe that «intellect is what it is», but in truth, especially about dogs, that's not the case. According to the last studies, we find three types of intelligence:

- Adaptive intelligence. This kind of intelligence allows a dog to adapt to unknown situations, and it can be improved by teaching new things or exposing the dog to circumstances it is not used to, always with a positive, relaxed point of view.

- Instinctive intelligence, in which the dog follows its instincts: eat when it's hungry, sleep when it's tired, pee when it's needed... This kind of intelligence must be trained and improved, for example, to teach it where to pee, or to gain self-control.
- Functional intelligence, which has a lot to do with the breed itself, and the predisposition of certain breeds for certain tasks. In a nutshell, this is the reason why a Beagle may learn quickly how to be a good hunter, while a Maltese will need more time.

To Stimulate Its Intellect

You need to keep in mind those different types of intelligence in order to stimulate the intellect of your Lagotto Romagnolo, but you also need to know and use some instincts and natural needs. Those needs are:

- Food
- Shelter
- Company
- Rules
- Routine

It's quite easy to provide for the first and second items, and only some people are negligent with the third. However, the last two give a good amount of problems, since we are not prepared to provide those rules, routines and training a dog actually NEEDS.

However, without this training, your Lagotto Romagnolo will not improve in behavior or intelligence. And to actually train it, you will probably need some of the methods I'm going to show you about stimulating its intellect.

In these pages, I'm going to teach you five different methods, each one harder than the last, but all of them linked to dog needs and dog training.

So, are you ready? Let's start with the easiest one.

Method 1: Interactive Toys

This is the easiest way to stimulate Your Lagotto Romagnolo's intelligence, although not the best. Interactive toys allow you to be freer: you just need to give them to Your Lagotto Romagnolo, maybe teach it to use them, and then you can just let it play while you go to work, shopping or preparing a meal.

Of course, there is a limit in the usefulness of toys; on the other hand, they go beyond the intellect of your Lagotto Romagnolo. But let me explain.

Usefulness

Interactive toys, and toys in general, serve a bigger purpose than only to make a dog smarter. Some examples of what you can accomplish with the correct toys are...

- Separation anxiety. If Your Lagotto Romagnolo is entertained with something, then it is not thinking about how much it misses you and how scary it is to be left alone. So, there is a lesser chance for it to bark or chew things when you are not there.
- Distraction. Dogs can be very demanding, so when you are in an important dinner, or cleaning, or when you come from work very tired and just want to watch the TV, your little fur friend comes and

wants attention and to play. Toys are useful to distract it, so Your Lagotto Romagnolo will be entertained for a while.

- Problem resolution. There are actual, real puzzles for dogs that they need to handle in a certain way in order to get a treat. This forces the dog to try different ways to get the prize.
- Sense stimulation. Some toys have the special function of stimulating the senses of Your Lagotto Romagnolo, especially smell.

Some of those toys are...

The variety is really huge, but I'm going to name a few of those interactive toys. I want to tell you what they are and what's their purpose.

Scent carpet

Quite an explicative name. This carpet has stripes or even synthetic fur; you need to put on them an attractive smell, with sprays, fresh grass or even rubbing treats on them. You can use different scents in different parts of the rug.

The goal is to have Your Lagotto Romagnolo entertained with so many fascinating odors, that it may be hours smelling its favorite rug. Moreover! It could help to teach it a few new words, for example, «grass», and let him sniff the portion of the carpet with the grass smell.

Dental Brush

There is a special brush for dogs, one you put in your finger to rub Your Lagotto Romagnolo's teeth, but now I'm talking about something different: it's literally a toy, but it helps to clean the teeth, so you can avoid flights, fears or bites.

Until now, I saw two different kinds, like a stick or like a ball, but both have gaps where you can put edible pastooth for dogs, or even treats, if it is big enough.

Intelligent Dispenser

Wonderful for voracious dogs, but also to control anxiety and stimulate intellect. Those dispensers can be mechanics or very simple, in which case are bowls with a kind of labyrinth, so the food will be a little difficult to reach.

The dog has to move around, chew and turn to get it.

Teach Your Lagotto Romagnolo How to Use Them!

*This is useful for both normal and interactive toys.

You may have noticed that sometimes Your Lagotto Romagnolo just ignores its toys, or at most carries them here and there, but nothing else. However, it seems that Your Lagotto Romagnolo is always chewing your shoes or destroying your furniture... which has no sense, right?

Most of the time, the reason for this odd behavior is quite simple: the dog doesn't recognize the toy as such. That's because we tend to give our dogs different objects, but we do not teach them how to actually use them. Some people think that that's absurd... A dog knows veeeery well how to chew your shoes, right? But here is the thing: there is nothing, absolutely nothing in their instincts that says that this round object is made specially for them to play with. That's something dogs need to *learn*.

Luckily, it's quite easy. We need only to poke those same instincts:

- Move the toy near Your Lagotto Romagnolo. This will poke the hunter's instinct with the fast movement one side and the other.
- When Your Lagotto Romagnolo takes or chew a toy, reward it with good pets or sweet words. Avoid treats, since you want its mouth to be well occupied with the toy.
- Don't scold it for chewing what it shouldn't! Say "no" with conviction, but don't yell, and offer a toy. When it chews the toy, then reward it. This is called "redirect bad behavior", and it's the best way to completely avoid them.
- Don't scold Your Lagotto Romagnolo if you see your things chewed

everywhere: it will not connect the object with the chewing it did an hour back. So, in summary, scolding will serve no purpose.

Final Goal

The final goal of those interactive toys is to give a good independent entertainment to Your Lagotto Romagnolo. In other words, those toys are useful to keep it distracted for a while, alone, and most of the time they help it to think, which will improve its intelligence. However, keep in mind that the usefulness of those toys, no matter how advanced or interactive they were, is limited. To really improve Your Lagotto Romagnolo's intellect you need to be a little bit more involved.

Extra tip: Cycle Your Toys

As a last tip on this topic, think about the possibility to cycle the toys for Your Lagotto Romagnolo. As an example, give it three or four toys, but in a month change them for another three or four, and the next month, change again.

This will make the toys always something new, so a dog doesn't feel bored, and doesn't get used to them.

Method 2: Treasure Quest

Searching is part of a dog's very nature: be it tracking or hunting, its sense of smell is an essential tool for all it was born to —don't forget that dogs descend from wolves, some of the best hunters of nature—.

Making good use of this impulse of tracking and looking for objects or prey will help you not only to improve its intellect facing obstacles, but also its senses and obedience. There are a lot of games that focus exactly on that.

Some common plays like fetch the ball or pull the rope would be useful, but I want to talk about hide-and-seek and some of its variants, since those plays greatly improve the intellect of any dog.

That's what I call Treasure Quest.

How to Teach It

Previously, it's a good idea that Your Lagotto Romagnolo knows and follows the order "stay", so you can hide the treasure. But we will talk about tricks later.

- Show the treasure to Your Lagotto Romagnolo, one that it really likes. To start, it's a good idea to use food or treats.
- Hide it, but not too much. It's ok if Your Lagotto Romagnolo sees you

while you hide the treasure, and if it is in plain sight. That's why it's a good thing that Your Lagotto Romagnolo can stay "quiet" in the meantime.

- When the treasure is hidden —even if it's in plain sight the first few times—, you can "release" your Lagotto Romagnolo and order it to "search", or the order you want to use. Since the treasure is visible, Your Lagotto Romagnolo will jump towards it.

- When the treasure is found, be happy and reward with pets and with a big, big party for the success!

Now now, I think this seems silly. If Your Lagotto Romagnolo sees what it has to search, what's the point? Well, the point is that you are teaching it to look for something when you tell it to do so. In order words, you are teaching an order.

- Repeat the process a few times. After some successes, it's time to hide the treasure. It can't be in plain sight like before, but the place should be easy enough to find and reach.
- Order Your Lagotto Romagnolo to search. This time will be difficult, but not too much.
- Again, make a huge party for every success!

Now your Lagotto Romagnolo can't see the treasure, but it KNOWS where it is, because it saw you hide it... now Your Lagotto Romagnolo needs to follow the trail: "I can't see it, but I know it's in there".

- After a few more repetitions, you can make it a bit more difficult. The most important part is that your Lagotto Romagnolo can't follow you when you hide the treasure: it can't know where it is. So you show your treasure, let Your Lagotto Romagnolo smell it, then go to another room and hide it... but easy, like on the floor or over a table.
- Release Your Lagotto Romagnolo and order it to search.
- Normally now, the dog will go to the room where you hide the treasure, but if not, no problem: let it smell

everywhere and look where it wants.

- When the treasure is found, party! It's very, very important that every little success was something big.

If your Lagotto Romagnolo loses the trail and gets frustrated, don't worry. Try calling it near the treasure —but it's important that it comes when you call—. This way, it will see you but also the treasure, which it will get right away.

Avoid frustration. It's a game, and Your Lagotto Romagnolo must find it funny and interesting, not a source of uneasiness.

- It's time for the acid test: now you really hide the treasure... another room, behind furniture, even inside a drawer!

To this point, it would be a really good thing that Your Lagotto Romagnolo barks when you order.

So, let me explain: your Lagotto Romagnolo sniffs around the place where the treasure is, and you order it to bark, you are teaching that finding the right spot means one bark which means a reward.

Some Variants

There are alternative options to this game. For example, you may teach Your Lagotto Romagnolo to look for you, so the game is transformed into Hide and Seek. It's quite simple, really, all you have to do is hide and then call your Lagotto Romagnolo. Using a specific order, like "look for me" would be good.

Another option, one I really like, is quite easy. Do you know about those street performance, where one hide a coin under a glass, then moves it and two others, and then another has to say where the coin is? Well... You know what? Your Lagotto Romagnolo can do that too! Try showing it a treat, then hide it under a glass, then move them... This way Your Lagotto Romagnolo will be using its senses, specially sight and smell.

Another, even easier alternative, is to hide a treat in your hand, show Your Lagotto Romagnolo both fists —changing the treat to the other hand, or not, that's up to you— and wait to see if your Lagotto Romagnolo discovers where it is.

Final Goal

In the end, all those games have the same goal: to stimulate the senses and mind of a dog: the thrill of the chase and the search of a treasure lead dogs to pay attention to detail, like smell or something in an odd place. The more difficult, the more stimulating.

Method 3: Training

Not everything can be about toys and play, even when Your Lagotto Romagnolo understands it like so. In fact, this is the idea you need to keep in mind when you get actually serious.

Sure, it's possible that you have been thinking something like... there's no use in training Your Lagotto Romagnolo, it is not exactly clever, and that's the reason why you are reading this: to make it smarter, so you can train it. Well, you are right... but only partially.

In truth, training and canine intelligence are closely related, because the first drives to the later.

What is Dog Training?

It would be better to start with: what is NOT dog training.

Dog Training is NOT about yelling at your Lagotto Romagnolo.

Training is NOT to hit it.

It is NOT ordering it around WITHOUT teaching anything.

So the well-known rolled-up newspaper is useless, like locking up Your Lagotto Romagnolo in a room, yelling when it barks or scolding it saying "bad dog" —your Lagotto Romagnolo just doesn't understand.

So, the training I want to talk about is what's called Positive Training, or also Relationship Training. It's based on the bond between you and Your Lagotto Romagnolo, and on rewarding every good behavior while the bad one is redirected, not punished.

Bases for Dog Training

I'm not going to stay for long here, since this is about improving Your Lagotto Romagnolo's intellect, but I want to tell you some basics so you can train it and help it improve. Remember! Training and intelligence always go together.

Basic Needs of a Dog

In any good training, you need to keep in mind the needs of your Lagotto Romagnolo to use them in your favor. I'm not going to dwell in shelter or medical care, since those are surely known to you. However, I'm going to focus on other needs that would be really useful in training:

- Food is the first motor of a dog's behavior. Rewards in the form of treats, something it really likes, are always the best... although not the only option.

- Interaccion. Your Lagotto Romagnolo needs to be in contact with you, with other people, with animals and with its surroundings. An isolated dog is a sad dog that can start to lose energy until it is extinguished, or can be hyperactive, erratic and aggressive. So playing with Your Lagotto Romagnolo, talking to it, or just petting it, all of those are rewards as strong and useful as food.

- Stimulus, or in other words, all that keeps Your Lagotto Romagnolo entertained and distracted. Stimulus can be games, toys, smells, movement... it comes from everywhere, and that's the main reason why walking Your Lagotto Romagnolo is so important, since the street is filled with stimulus which are basic for the good psychological development of any dog, no matter its age, and they are also quite useful in dog training.

Rules, Consistency and Constancy

To train your Lagotto Romagnolo, you need to know the rules you want it to follow. Think it through, because they are very important: rules need to be stable, consistent, they can't be changing over time.

Here's a simple example: You tell Your Lagotto Romagnolo it can't jump on the sofa. It tries, but you fetch it off. Well, you are not going to allow it anymore, so that's ok. However, the next day Your Lagotto Romagnolo tries again, and then you are so tired of working that you just let it be, for once. And so your Lagotto Romagnolo thinks...

"hey! Today I can do it, so maybe tomorrow too".

Like that, a dog never learns, because there's always the possibility of "tomorrow".

Some questions you would want to ask yourself about the rules of your house are...

- Can Your Lagotto Romagnolo jump on the sofa?
- And on the bed?
- Can Your Lagotto Romagnolo go to the street alone?
- Can it pull the leash when walking?
- Can it ask for food when you eat?
- Can it ignore its own food to ask you for something else?
- Can it bark at every sound?
- Can it chase cars or animals?
- Can it chew shoes or furniture?
- Can it growl?

Good Mood

And I'm not talking about your Lagotto Romagnolo, but about you: it's important that YOU keep control over yourself and your frustrations and anxieties, that you don't yell and make sudden moves. It's vital that Your Lagotto Romagnolo sees you as calm and serene, so you always need to be relaxed and secure.

I know, that's not easy, but a secure, firm human makes a dog also like that: they catch the same energy, relax, and then it's easier for them to learn and obey.

Reward the Good Behavior

This is quite easy. When your Lagotto Romagnolo does something you like, just reward it: use treats, pets, happy words, toys or games. There are many things you can use.

Redirecting Bad Behavior

This is perhaps the hardest part of the training: you CANNOT punish bad behavior, since it would produce fear unease, which never helps in any learning.

Instead of that, you can redirect, or even ignore!, those bad behaviors. Here there are some examples:

- Your Lagotto Romagnolo chews your shoes. You say "no!", a word that Your Lagotto Romagnolo will relate to things not ok, and then you give it a toy. When Your Lagotto Romagnolo chews the toy, you pet it and say well done.

- Your Lagotto Romagnolo barks. Say "no!" and give it a toy or a treat, something to keep its mouth occupied, so when the dog stops barking, you can give a new order, like "quiet", so it will relate keeping quiet with the instruction with the reward.

- Your Lagotto Romagnolo begs when you eat. Ignore it. It's very hard, but don't make a sound, don't look at it, don't pet it, NEVER give it a piece of food. In the end, your Lagotto Romagnolo will understand it's no use, and so it will stop begging.

The Most Important Thing

To train your Lagotto Romagnolo, the most important thing is repetition: keep rewarding good behavior, keep ignoring or redirecting the bad. Be consistent, consequent, don't falter nor change the rules.

This way, Your Lagotto Romagnolo finally learns, and every time it understands something new, its intellect improves, so the next one will be even easier to get.

And like this, everythings is perfectly tied up.

Method 4: Tricks

Teaching things to dogs —or to any animal, even humans— is the best way to improve their intellect, especially with the correct rewards —which surely you already know—. Something truly useful to teach are tricks, since they are many, and very varied, and some of them are absolutely essential in the every-day life, while others are just so fun.

So, when you ask your Lagotto Romagnolo to learn something new, you are asking to focus, to memorize, to relate concepts, and all of that improves its intelligence. And when you ask it to repeat what it already knows, you make it remember, which really helps.

As you can see, tricks are an incredible way to improve their intellect, which is the final goal of this book. Now, you need to get very involved in it, as much as with the training. There is no halfway.

Previous Tips

There are a few things you must remember in order to teach tricks to your Lagotto Romagnolo:

- Repetition is key. The more times you repeat a trick, while Your Lagotto Romagnolo learns and after that, the better it will perform and the more easily it will remember.
- Dogs have a short scope of attention, so I recommend the

training sessions to be no longer than ten minutes.

- You can repeat a session twice a day, if you want, but never too close one to another. It would be ok if you have one session in the morning, and the other in the evening.
- Change the hour of training and also the place every few times.

How to Teach Tricks

The most basic shape to teach any trick would be:

- Lead Your Lagotto Romagnolo to do something —don't worry, I will explain later—.
- When the dog does what you want, give the order and the reward.
- Repeat a few times.

- Change the order: give the command. If Your Lagotto Romagnolo does not obey the first time, then repeat while you lead Your Lagotto Romagnolo to do what you want.
- When it does, reward.
- Repeat.
- And keep repeating until Your Lagotto Romagnolo obeys the first time you give the command.
- Reinforce the trick in different places.
- The sequence must always be:
  - Order
  - Obedience
  - Reward

As you can see, it's not hard. The key is always repetition.

Basic Tricks

These are a few tricks that are not only good, but essential in everyday life.

Come

This trick is so ESSENTIAL that it may well save the life of Your Lagotto Romagnolo. For example, calling it when it is on the street can avoid accidents, or even Your Lagotto Romagnolo getting lost. It can help Your Lagotto Romagnolo to avoid dangers that you can see, but it cannot.

Of course, it's also useful for less dangerous matters, like calling for the training session, or jumping in the car.

So to get started: Start in a place with little or no distractions, and use something that Your Lagotto Romagnolo likes, like a toy or a treat, so it will come to you. Make sure to give the order when Your Lagotto Romagnolo is coming, and reward when it arrives.

Sit

This is basic to teach most of the other tricks. It's a good idea that Your Lagotto Romagnolo starts with the sitting position, then changes to the next trick. Moreover, you can use "sit" to ask Your Lagotto Romagnolo to greet your visitors, or when you are dining outside.

To get started: Take a treat and close your fist around, then pass it over the head of your Lagotto Romagnolo and its back, very slowly, letting Your Lagotto Romagnolo follow your fist with its sight. The most probable outcome is that it will sit to keep looking, so you can give the order, reward.

Lay

This trick starts with "sit" and is about asking your Lagotto Romagnolo to lay down on the floor or the bed. This position helps it to relax, and it's useful if you are doing chores at home and you need Your Lagotto Romagnolo to be, you know, *not at your feet*.

To get started: begin with "sit" position, then take a treat, close the fist, and lower it slowly in front of Your Lagotto Romagnolo, to the ground. Your Lagotto Romagnolo will try to follow the movement —and probably touch your fist with its nose—, and to do that it will need to lay down.

Stop

With this order, you tell your Lagotto Romagnolo to stop moving, no matter what is happening. It's a basic trick for autocontrol: be it food on its plate, or you talking to the mailman, no matter what Your Lagotto Romagnolo needs to stay quiet if you say so.

To get started: from a sit or lay position, so Your Lagotto Romagnolo stays comfortable, order it to "stop" and wait one or two seconds. Give it the reward. It seems odd, but starting with very short times helps your Lagotto Romagnolo to understand the order. Then you can start to wait for three, five, ten seconds.

Stay

The natural evolution of "stop", with this other trick you can move away and do other things, and still Your Lagotto Romagnolo will stay put and wait for your commands. As an example, you can order it to stay while you mop the floor, or you can play hide.

However, never ask Your Lagotto Romagnolo to stay put forever. It may forget quite easily why it was ordered. You need to "free" Your Lagotto Romagnolo, with words like "well done", "move" or even "come". Of course, you need to be consistent with this one too.

To get started: it's a must that Your Lagotto Romagnolo knows the "stop" command. Then you say "stop, stay", and take a step backwards. If Your Lagotto Romagnolo stays, free and reward it. If it moves, try again with a shorter step.

Heel

Very useful when you walk, this trick tells your Lagotto Romagnolo to stay at your side —right or left, whatever you chose to teach it—, so you both can walk without pulling.

To get started: take a reward in one hand, at your side. Say "heel" and show Your Lagotto Romagnolo the treat, but give it only when Your Lagotto Romagnolo is correctly positioned at your side.

Quiet

Very useful with barking dogs, this tells them that it's time to be quiet. This trick is really useful with dogs that suffer from compulsive barking.

To get started: when Your Lagotto Romagnolo barks, you say "quiet" and then offer something to occupy its mouth, like a treat or a toy. Don't give it immediately, however, only after a second or so of silence, so Your Lagotto Romagnolo will understand that being quiet is actually quite beneficious.

Advanced Tricks

Also "funny tricks", there are a lot of absolutely wonderful tricks for your Lagotto Romagnolo to show its intellect and good behavior. But beware! Those are quite difficult to teach and to learn.

Paw

This trick is more funny than useful, and it's just about Your Lagotto Romagnolo raising its paw and putting it on your hand, allowing you to shake. You can even ask the other paw afterwards.

To get started: show Your Lagotto Romagnolo a treat and close the fist. It will touch with its nose and, eventually, with its paw. When your Lagotto Romagnolo does, give the order and let it take the treat.

Greet

It is a variant of the paw trick, and for me even better. Picture this: your cousins comes to your home for dinner, and your Lagotto Romagnolo goes to them, sits and raises a paw like saying "hey, what's up!". So adorable!

To get started: When Your Lagotto Romagnolo already knows the paw trick, just ask it "paw", then help it to lift it a little while saying "greet", then reward.

Another option: really well trained dogs will try to imitate you if you lift your hand. Try it!

Play dead

Who doesn't know this trick? It is about Your Lagotto Romagnolo laying down on the floor as if being hit by a bullet.
They can be really good at acting!

To get started: From lay position, get the reward in your first and move to right or left, so your Lagotto Romagnolo finally gets on its side.

Roll

The natural evolution of the previous one, Your Lagotto Romagnolo needs to roll on the floor after laying down.

To get started: After your Lagotto Romagnolo successfully lies on one side, just keep going, luring with treats to roll.

Bark

The natural evolution of telling Your Lagotto Romagnolo to keep quiet is to ask it to bark... in a controlled way, when you say. You can even teach it to bark a specific number of times.

In the same sense, you can teach it basic arithmetic, like three plus two. A well trained dog that knows the trick and has a well developed intellect would be able to bark five times. But don't increase the numbers too much! We know dogs can count up to ten, but we don't know more.

To get started: you need to find an stimulus that makes it bark, and use it. You can also wait for Your Lagotto Romagnolo to bark but itself. In any case, when it does, give the order and reward, then it will keep quiet to eat the treat.

Treat over the nose

An evolution of «stop» and «stay» is to ask Your Lagotto Romagnolo to be still while you put a treat over its nose, and it can't move until you say so. Perfection is really difficult to achieve: the final goal is that, when you order it, Your Lagotto Romagnolo will lift its head and take the treat in the air. You both need lots of patience and no little skill!

To get started: it is very important to know the «stop» command perfectly. Give the order, put the treat over its nose, wait a second or two, then allow it to move and eat.

Under the bridge

This trick is for your Lagotto Romagnolo to pass between your legs at your order.
It's very common in talent shows or agility competitions.

To get started: open your legs and show Your Lagotto Romagnolo a treat between them, luring it to pass under them.

Get up

A funny trick for your Lagotto Romagnolo to get up on its back legs. However, keep in mind that they are not biped, so this trick must be really short to avoid back problems.

To get started: from «sit» position, raise your hand swiftly with a treat on it, luring Your Lagotto Romagnolo to get up. Start by rewarding when Your Lagotto Romagnolo lifts one paw.

Touch

The theory is quite simple: it's about your Lagotto Romagnolo learning to touch certain objects with its nose or paw.

This trick, however, can be very ample, and you can teach it to recognize very different objects, to the point where Your Lagotto Romagnolo would be able to sound specific bells to communicate different things, like «hungry», «pee» or «bored».

To get started: from the «sit» position, offer your fist to Your Lagotto Romagnolo. When your Lagotto Romagnolo touches it, give the order and reward.

Step

A very nice trick that allows you both to show up your group effort. It's about you and your Lagotto Romagnolo walking at the same time, like in a military march: when you raise your left leg, Your Lagotto Romagnolo raises its left paw, and the same with the right.

To get started: from standing position, offer your fist with a treat, so Your Lagotto Romagnolo will touch it. When your Lagotto Romagnolo lifts one paw, say «left» or «right», and reward. It's important that Your Lagotto Romagnolo relates the order with the specific paw.

Method 5: Tracks

This is the «grand finale», the most difficult method, but also the best suited to stimulate the intelligence of your Lagotto Romagnolo. You really need to have some background in training and tricks before trying this one. Tracks are sequences of obstacles used in agility competitions, but you can make them in a park or just at home. Your furniture can be just perfect, creating a path filled with chairs, tables or boxes so your Lagotto Romagnolo has to jump or crouch or roll to pass through.

Obviously, you need the space and the material to make the tracks. If Your Lagotto Romagnolo is little or young, that's easy, since a bit of cardboard and a decent dining room would be enough to create a perfect labyrinth. You can do the same for bigger dogs, of course, but you need more space.

I can't tell you what kind of track to make at home, since it depends on everything: your own furniture, space, time, materials... and your will. But I can say that imagination is everything: even your bedroom can be a wonderful track. An example could be...

- Cross under a bridge
- Up to a seesaw
- Down from the other side
- Through a tunel
- Jump an obstacle
- Turn

- Zigzag around a line of cones
- Turn
- Jump over a platform
- Get down and crouch under a low obstacle
- Run
- Seesaw
- Cross the finish line
-

As I said, that's only an example. Variations are just infinite, your imagination is the limit. But you need to tell Your Lagotto Romagnolo what to do in every step of the track, and your Lagotto Romagnolo has to memorize every order and action.

Indeed, that's not easy! But, by a lot, this is the final test in canine intellect. Of course, that's also a lot of work... and a very strong bond between you two.

How To Potty Train Your Lagotto Romagnolo More Effectively

Bringing an adult dog into your home demands as much effort from you and the family as does a puppy. It's a mistake to think that just because the dog is full-grown and may have been potty trained in one home, that he'll just immediately adjust to your home's elimination schedule, too.

That's not realistic. The dog has many adjustments to his new environment and doesn't instinctively know that you don't allow peeing on the floor – especially his prior owner didn't mind or didn't seem to care.

Don't make the mistake of assuming that because he's an adult dog that he'll just "know" what to do.
Start with him as if he were a puppy and gradually teach him the routine of your home's pet potty schedule.

You probably need to start with crate training or restriction to a bathroom. Then set a schedule for potty breaks. Adult dogs are very picky about finding a potty place outside that's apart from where they play, just as they don't like to potty near where they sleep or eat.

Help him find that place in your yard or outside when walking and return him there for subsequent potty breaks. You have to monitor the potty breaks for several weeks to learn elimination patterns of your Lagotto Romagnolo.

You also have to set morning and evening feeding times. He may not have had such an organized life schedule, so this could take time for adjustment.

Don't believe that old saying, 'you can't teach an old dog new tricks." It's not the age of the dog that matters - it's the consistency of the owner.

If Your Lagotto Romagnolo came from an abusive home, even if is was just filled with shouting and hitting with paper for any accidents, then your training efforts may take longer. First you have to win the dog's confidence and understand that he needs time to get comfortable in his new home.

There will be accidents, so be prepared to clean it up and move forward. Don't assume that an adult dog will be any easier to train than a puppy. Both dogs would face the same adjustment issues. You have to train with consistency and affection so that you reinforce the responses that you want repeated.

An older male dog may be accustomed to marking his territory by urinating on it. This is an instinctive behavior for male dogs - you aren't going to break him of it without breaking his spirit or having him neutered.

Consistency Is Key with Housetraining

There are very few dogs that can't be housetrained - just poor pet owners who don't understand the value of consistency. You're the most important element in successful housetraining for a puppy or adult dog that's new in your home.

The dog is looking to you to set boundaries and rules, while also showing that he's welcome in your world.

Housetraining might take a few days – or it might take months – each dog is different.

It takes at least several weeks or a few months to establish housetraining with a puppy. Some owners say that puppies are easier to train, since they have no negative experiences to counteract.

Other owners insist that an older dog is easier to train because they have better developed bladders, can wait longer between breaks and know something about housetraining. It doesn't matter which is right or wrong, it's only about dealing with the dog you have in the most positive way so that you're teaching a good lesson, not instilling fear.

The old method of housebreaking was punishment centered hitting a puppy with rolled up paper to make him stop having accidents and then punishing him again because he urinated on the floor instead of the newspaper.

Needless to say, it rarely got the desired behavior. Positive reinforcement shows the puppy exactly what you want him to do by rewarding the potty behavior with praise and affection.

These are far more powerful motivators for Your Lagotto Romagnolo than punishment. If Your Lagotto Romagnolo senses that you're going to be home soon, he will make every effort to wait for the potty break.

But if you're home on time one day, late the next and later the following day, then Your Lagotto Romagnolo is smart enough to give up and go when he has to.

That's not his choice - particularly if he's in a crate because he dislikes combining his potty with his personal space.

Losing that consistency will cause him to give up and go against his instinct to potty in separate place.

Housetraining takes time, so you need to be prepared to schedule yourself for this task until it's complete.

That's going to interrupt your schedule and cause you to watch the clock. If you'll make this sacrifice for the weeks needed to train Your Lagotto Romagnolo, then you'll be done with the process completely.

This is a small price to pay for a housetrained, well- adjusted dog that will live comfortably in your home for many years.
At the end of the training period, you aren't a screaming wreck and Your Lagotto Romagnolo isn't cowering under furniture at the sound of your voice. Effective training builds a lasting bond with Your Lagotto Romagnolo.

Crate Training Is the Most Common Potty Training Approach for Pups

Placing a puppy in a crate may sound restrictive and unkind, but when used positively, it can be effective for housetraining. By nature, dogs don't like to potty in the same place that they sleep or eat.

Now you know why the newspaper you put in the kitchen next to the dog bowls isn't as appealing for a potty as your living room carpet.

Crate training only gets the desired response if done when you're at home and supervising the time limits.

Confining a puppy in a crate while you're at work all day defeats the purpose. Unable to hold the urine, the puppy will potty in the crate and lose that natural instinct to separate the potty place from sleeping and eating spots.

By keeping the puppy in the crate for limited time, when you release him, he'll be ready and willing to potty where you say to go. That's when you want to be ready to take the puppy outside or bring him to the location where you have potty paper.

If the puppy soils inside the crate, make sure you clean it up before returning the puppy to the crate. Otherwise, you will set back your housetraining efforts. You have to be consistent in the times that you take the puppy out for a potty break.

With a puppy, don't go longer than an hour and half to two hours at the most so you can reinforce that going to the potty happens in a certain location, not just anywhere. If the dog quickly does his business, reward him enthusiastically with praise.

You may add a food treat – however, it's a good idea to offer different reinforcements for specific activities. Doggy cookies are great, but your affection and approval is by far the reward that Your Lagotto Romagnolo wants the most.

Unless you have a fenced yard, you can also use these frequent potty breaks to reinforce walking on the leash. Don't roam aimlessly during potty breaks. Give the dog five minutes to do the job, and then go back inside.

That will teach the dog that casual walks are just for fun, but potty walks are short and purposeful. You'll be glad you taught that lesson when the dog wakes you up at 3 o'clock in the morning in a desperate need to potty when the outside temperature is freezing.

To help you monitor the crate training, keep a log of times Your Lagotto Romagnolo spends in the crate and how often you take the dog out. In the beginning, you may need to take the dog out every 45 minutes to an hour for short breaks.

When you find that this is working, extend the time by 15- 20 minutes each period. In a few weeks, you'll learn the times of day the dog most commonly needs to potty and how long he can wait between breaks.

Don't punish him for having accidents. Simply revise the training schedule to shorten the time between potty breaks. If Your Lagotto Romagnolo fails to potty after several breaks, be smart and restrict his access to a kitchen or bathroom.

You don't want a dog with a full bladder to start active play or get excited. Those distractions often result in accidents.
After a successful potty break, you can give full run of the house as an additional reward. This will train the dog to see that after potty, he gets to have fun with the family, which is another reward.

Cruel House Training Tactics Are Out

If you bring home a puppy, be prepared to deal with accidents during the potty training phase. It's shocking the way people use abusive tactics to stop a puppy from doing what comes naturally.

Puppies are no more prepared to be instantly potty trained than human infants are. A period of development needs to be reached before the puppy is ready to follow your requests and commands.

The puppy desperately wants to please you and doesn't understand why he's being punished. The old views of punishment as a means of potty training are as outdated for dogs as they are for children. It simply doesn't work.

Rubbing a puppy's nose in the feces isn't a good approach. The dog only sees you as a tormentor and doesn't understand what you do want instead. There is a very real risk of serious illness to the puppy after getting a nose full of E-coli bacteria. If you're unhappy with the cost of having your rug cleaned, wait until you see the vet bill from an illness you caused!

Another type of fear-based potty training is to swat the dog with a rolled up newspaper after rubbing his nose in the feces. If the puppy could speak, he would say, "What makes you think I'm going to potty on newspaper in the kitchen after you hit me with it? I don't want anything to do with newspaper!" Hitting a puppy with rolled up newspaper merely teaches him to fear newspaper. You simply have to accept that a puppy will make mistakes. Sometimes, you're responsible for those mistakes. When you arrive home late or sleep in rather than taking the puppy outside, what you do expect him to do?

Don't punish the puppy because you changed the schedule. If you want to get the puppy accustomed to a morning and afternoon walking regimen, then you have to be consistent. You also have to respond when the puppy shows signs of discomfort, irritation or other means of trying to get your attention.

If he needs to g out, be fair. Don't you have days when your potty breaks are more frequent and sudden? What if you had an intense need to potty but your boss demanded that you sit though an hour-long meeting?

Be careful when training a puppy that you teach positive skills rather than instill fear at how mean you are. Too often the dog owner's frustration simply teaches a puppy to stay away. If a dog becomes mean, chances are he learned it from a mean spirited owner.

A puppy's world is playful, enthusiastic and adventure- filled. Sometimes chasing down that rubber ball is so intense that he forgets about going to the potty until his little bladder can't wait any longer and there's an accident. It wasn't on purpose, so be careful how you respond. A puppy with a broken spirit learns to watch for an open door to run away and never return.

Don't Let Your Puppy Get Used to Making Messes

When it comes to reducing household messes, your puppy can be easier to housetrain than a teenager. That's because a puppy - by nature - can't stand to live in the same area with his messes.

You can use that instinct to housetrain your puppy with minimal distress for both of you. A puppy that comes into your home directly from the breeder has adjustments that you have to consider.

Not only is the puppy in a strange environment, but he's been taken from his mother and siblings.

Where there were lots of little barks and playful activity among other puppies, he is now an "only dog" in a home where he must wait for your time and attention.

If your home is filled with children, then the puppy can actually be overwhelmed with attention and not enough time to rest. Be mindful that your little puppy has many adjustments to make in becoming part of your home and family.

If you're crate training your puppy, everyone in the home needs to agree that this job is under the control of one person or at least kept on a schedule.

Otherwise, the whimpering puppy in the crate might be released by a well meaning child (or another adult) and suddenly, there's a mess on the floor.

Worse still is to wake up in the predawn hours of the morning to take the puppy out for a break, only to have to go looking for the puppy.

Someone weakened and put the puppy in the bed. Unfortunately, the puppy needs to potty and the next pillow is as good as anyplace. Lesson learned - at least the lesson for the owners.

You may have to train the family at the same time you are training the puppy. Explain how the dog's instinct is to avoid doing potty business where he sleeps and eats.

That's why crate training is a kind of aversion therapy - so that the puppy will want to hold it until he's taken outside for official potty time.

Then make sure that you don't let your puppy spend time in his own mess inside the crate. If you constantly interrupt the housetraining routine, your puppy learns that you're not dependable and he accepts living in mess.

Once that happens, you lose weeks' worth of effort. So take advantage of the puppy's instinct for separating his life functions. Who knows - maybe this will rub off on your teenager!

Don't Scold, But Use Positive Reinforcement Instead

Have you ever noticed that as soon as you start fussing, your puppy hangs his little head and tucks his tail between his legs in despair? He knows you're upset and has no idea what to do about it.

If it's because of his "accident" on the floor, he's really confused. He had to potty and you weren't there to take him out - or you were too busy on the computer to stop and notice his needs.

At some point his bladder couldn't take it anymore and now he has your attention, but in a negative way. Scolding a puppy (or even an adult dog) that is new to your home for accidents is useless.

All you're teaching is that you have a short temper and your love is conditional. You don't show what you want him to do, so nothing is learned. Positive reinforcement focuses on teaching what you want the puppy to do instead of shouting about what you don't want.

With positive reinforcement, the puppy makes the association between what he just did and your praise. Since he desperately wants to please you, he tries to do it again for your approval.

With each reinforcement, the behavior becomes more and more automatic so the housetraining takes hold. Accidents happen - even to a dog that's housetrained. Upsets in the routine, visitors, home remodeling, and holiday schedules are just a few times that can cause Your Lagotto Romagnolo to be confused about what's expected.

When you find an accident, clean it up. Never rub his nose in it or scold him verbally.

If Your Lagotto Romagnolo seems to go to a certain place, like a lesser-used dining room to potty, then restrict access to that room by closing the door or putting up a child's gate.

If Your Lagotto Romagnolo has recently been left at a kennel for days or weeks, you may need to repeat the earlier crate training and provide more frequent potty breaks.

Do as you did when he was a puppy and make a chart of these breaks so that you can predict the dog's elimination patterns and intentionally time his breaks closer to them.

Your Lagotto Romagnolo depends on you to give him the potty opportunity when he needs it. Your Lagotto Romagnolo will go when he needs to, so make sure his potty break meets those times. When accidents look like diarrhea, Your Lagotto Romagnolo is having stomach upset not trying to defy you.

Don't punish him for what he can't prevent. Check the dog food. Is it out of date? Have you left dog food out for several hours? That can be a food danger. Make sure that no one in the family is feeding table scraps or junk food to the dog.

These are not suitable for the dog and can easily lead to stomach upset. Just as with humans, diarrhea or other sudden change in bowel habits can mean that Your Lagotto Romagnolo has a medical problem. You'll feel horribly guilty if you scold Your Lagotto Romagnolo, only to learn he couldn't control the potty problem.

Housebreaking Versus Housetraining

Housebreaking a puppy starts with the wrong premise – breaking.
It's as if you want to make the puppy stop being a puppy and function like a perfect little toy. That's neither fair nor realistic.

A pet owner who wants to establish a positive relationship with the pet is focused on housetraining. This approach shows the puppy how to live comfortably in your environment.

Forget the old school methods that teach you to start paper training and swatting a puppy the first day it's home.

Whether you bring home a puppy or an adult dog, you're taking this animal from the environment it knows and going into an environment that's totally foreign to it.

The dog has no idea what room is okay to go in and what room is off limits. A shelter dog or crated puppy is so excited to have space to walk and freedom to roam that your home is a virtual theme park of wonders. Add to that the presence of other pets or children and the excitement is almost too much to contain.

Housetraining takes a lot of your time. You need to work with Your Lagotto Romagnolo in every room. If the living room is off limits and you notice him sniffing for a place to potty, then gently pick him up, say "No" firmly without shouting, and then place him on the floor of the kitchen with his newspapers or take him outside.

You may have to do that dozens of times until he gets the message, but it will happen. Make sure you balance the "no-no" spaces with the "yes" spaces. Once Your Lagotto Romagnolo has learned the essential house rules for potty zones, you still have to allow for the unexpected.

A dog, particularly a puppy, who is alone and frightened by a thunderstorm or other loud noises may have a potty accident.

Or there may be a medical issue that requires you attention. Like humans, dogs can get urinary tract infections that make bladder control difficult.

A sudden change in potty training levels can be a cue that Your Lagotto Romagnolo's behavior change is from a physical problem, not defiance.
As Your Lagotto Romagnolo ages, bladder control will fail just as it does for many aging humans.

Any drastic change in routine can get Your Lagotto Romagnolo off his potty training path to success, too. Visiting relatives, home remodeling or emotional distress are all factors that can cause a dog to be lax in housetraining.

Think about what's going on around the home as possible reasons why the dog is feeling confused about what's happening around him and responding erratically. Restore order as you patiently go back and reinforce housetraining in positive ways.

Potty Training for Small Dogs

Granted, small dogs can only make small messes.

But you'll pay the same carpet cleaning costs to do the room with urine stains whether it's made by a Chihuahua or a Doberman. Small dogs need the same potty training basics as any dog.

You have to remember that their size might work against them in that their tiny bladders won't hold as much (or for as long) if you're late coming home for their potty break. Small dogs don't mind living in apartments or homes without big yards. They only need a little spot to do their business, so a flowerbed might be enough room.

Some people make fun of little dogs in their knit sweaters, but it's more than just a fashion statement. During the winter months in cold climates, the change from heated indoors to freezing outdoors is very harsh on a small dog's body.

The sudden chill can also distract them from the potty business and cause them to run back inside. Once warm again, the urge hits and there's nowhere to go but the rug. You can make this easier on your small dog by getting him a warm sweater for cold weather.

Some small dogs will not budge off their hind legs until they see the sweater in your hands. Your small dog may totally refuse to go outdoors in rain or cold, even with a sweater on. You have to plan options. Perhaps you can keep a papered box in the garage as a backup potty during bad weather. Only use this for limited times during the year so that you don't discourage the dog from going outside to his regular potty spots.

If your small dog goes outdoors in a yard or in the park, be alert as to where he's walking. Keep Your Lagotto Romagnolo away from tall grass or bushes. While he's busy trying to sniff out the right spot, he's easy prey for snakes in tall grass.

Owners of small dogs can become insensitive to their neighbors. Just because the feces is small, it's still dog poop. Pick it up - your neighbor didn't contract with your for fertilizer.

Not to mention that dog poop on their shoes may not be visible until it's tracked onto the carpet. That won't win you an invitation to the neighbor's next bar-b-q. It's your responsibility to clean up after Your Lagotto Romagnolo. Don't try to get out of it by arguing that it's so small it doesn't matter. It matters to anyone who doesn't own it.

Housetraining for small dogs is the same as for large dogs. You can begin with crate training and frequent breaks until a routine is established. Some small dogs can be temperamental because many are spoiled lap dogs. That's where the positive reinforcement of your praise and affection is even stronger - when it's so important to Your Lagotto Romagnolo to please you.

Setting a Schedule for Eliminations of Your Lagotto Romagnolo

As you housetrain Your Lagotto Romagnolo, you have to set up a schedule. Your Lagotto Romagnolo isn't going to do that for himself. It takes your effort and monitoring for several weeks to a few months for this to occur, so that Your Lagotto Romagnolo learns a routine.

You can help Your Lagotto Romagnolo know when it's the right time to go potty by repeating that routine consistently. When most people wake up, they usually go to the bathroom soon afterwards.

Well, Your Lagotto Romagnolo needs the same courtesy. Don't stop to make coffee or check the newspaper - take Your Lagotto Romagnolo out as soon as you're up and moving. He's been holding it all night, so don't make this difficult.

Keep the first potty break short, and then bring him inside for breakfast. Let Your Lagotto Romagnolo eat breakfast while you're getting dressed and ready for the day. By the time you finish your coffee and breakfast, you can take the dog out for a potty break.

If he's had some time to eat and let the food settle, he'll be ready for elimination before going into the crate or the room where he spends the day. With a puppy, you need to come back for a mid-day potty break and a mid-afternoon break if possible.

When you're at work, let another family member or willing neighbor handle those breaks for you. Just make sure everyone knows and follows the routine you use for breaks. Make the breaks short (5-10 minutes) and don't mix playtime with potty time. Your Lagotto Romagnolo needs to clearly understand the difference and he will - if you're consistent.

Keep the same routine for dinnertime. Let Your Lagotto Romagnolo out for a potty break as soon as you return home from work or school. Set a time to feed the dog and don't get more than thirty minutes off schedule.

It's better to feed the dog early in the evening, so that the food digests and he's ready for an elimination break before bedtime. Then follow the same procedure that you do in the morning.

As you're housetraining Your Lagotto Romagnolo, keep notes of the times. You can even create a simple checklist to post on the refrigerator. Then anyone who feeds the dog or takes him for potty breaks can make note of the time. This is helpful in noticing what the dog's natural elimination patterns are.

When Your Lagotto Romagnolo completes his potty break, remember to give him praise and affection. You can offer a dog biscuit, but it's not necessary.

He's just as happy with your approval. Instead of the old training methods that punish a dog for making a mess in the house, you take the more effective positive approach to show him approval for getting the job done during a scheduled potty break.

Since Your Lagotto Romagnolo wants you to love him, he will be willing to try his best to please you. Just don't make it difficult. If you're running late and miss his potty break, clean it up and get back on track without scolding him. Your Lagotto Romagnolo depends on you for many things, including staying on target for potty breaks. He doesn't want to mess in his space - or in yours - so help him do the right thing by sticking to a routine.

The Leash and Crate Mix

Most dogs lack the opportunity to roam a large backyard at will. They're more likely to spend the day indoors while their family members are away at work and school. This can make sticking to a potty training schedule more difficult.

A combination of crate and leash training works for some dogs. If the adult dog is new to your family or returning home after time in a kennel while you were away, you may have to reinforce his potty training.

One option is to return him to the crate during the day and possibly use a leash that's not overly restrictive when you're present so that he stays in one area of the home.
Keeping the dog contained 100% of the time isn't the total answer - it's merely part of the process.

Start as you would with a puppy and set up regular potty breaks. Make sure that you time the elimination breaks with enough time after feeding so the dog can do something meaningful on the trip outside.

Spend the weekend closely observing him on the leash whenever he's out of the crate so that you begin to recognize the signs that he needs to potty. He may shake, sniff around, act agitated or start to squat. Those are your signals to stop what you're doing and immediately take him to potty.

Remember to praise him lavishly when he does his business during the potty break. That's the positive reinforcement needed to show Your Lagotto Romagnolo where he's supposed to do his business.

If, during your absence, Your Lagotto Romagnolo stayed in a kennel where he eliminated, ate and slept in the same area, then he may have lost his earlier training. He's also probably very depressed and dejected.

Dogs don't like to mix potty with living space anymore than you want to eliminate on the floor in your kitchen. So he needs to start again and build up confidence in his potty skills and in the willingness of the adult on duty to take him out when he needs to go.

An older dog probably has better bladder control than a puppy, so he can usually go longer periods between potty breaks. However, Your Lagotto Romagnolo may have a urinary tract infection, diarrhea or other medical problem that's the real cause of his accidents.

If you see a noticeable change in Your Lagotto Romagnolo's potty behaviors and there are no other apparent reasons for it, then you want get him checked at the vet. The potty problems may be a symptom of a greater problem.

During the time he's being treated for the medical condition, go easy on the potty training. Your Lagotto Romagnolo needs to feel well and be reasonably able to manage his urine and elimination so that he can cooperate with your training.

Keep him on a leash when he's not in the crate and carefully care for him by helping notice signs that he needs to potty while he recovers.

Watch The Diet of Your Lagotto Romagnolo During the Housetraining Process

As Your Lagotto Romagnolo is learning to follow a potty break routine, you have to avoid doing anything that makes the lessons harder. One way you can help this process is in managing the dog's food intake.

As you monitor and log the crate time and potty breaks, you'll notice a pattern in Your Lagotto Romagnolo's elimination.
Make sure that the food you provide and the timing of feedings don't compromise training.

Feed Your Lagotto Romagnolo at the same time each day. If you feed him in the morning before leaving for work, put out the food as soon as you wake up. The dog can eat and begin to digest the food while you're getting dressed and having your breakfast.

Then the dog will be ready to potty before you leave. Never leave the dog food out all day. If Your Lagotto Romagnolo (especially a puppy) eats gradually all day long without a potty break, you're asking for an accident to happen.

For crate training a puppy, make sure there's a supply of water in a container that won't tip. Also leave a few small dog biscuits or treats in case he gets hungry during the day
- but don't leave a full meal.

When you get home, take the dog out and then feed him. Don't wait until late evening to feed dinner to the puppy or you'll be cleaning up feces in the crate or on the rug. Allow a reasonable time for the digestion to occur.

No matter how much the dog begs, don't give table scraps or snack foods. These are not well tolerated by most dogs and some snack foods can be harmful to the dog (and not so great for you either).

Just because a dog will eat what you give him in food scraps doesn't mean it's suitable for him. Feeding him the wrong kind of foods is likely to result in doggie diarrhea. If you don't give Your Lagotto Romagnolo the non-nutrient snacks and junk that you eat, he won't develop a taste for it - which is definitely better for everyone in the long run.

High quality dog food is made with added nutrients and designed for the age and weight of Your Lagotto Romagnolo. If you're on a budget, find a place to skimp besides Your Lagotto Romagnolo food budget. Cheap dog foods can contain ingredients that cause stomach upset and have minimal nutritional value, so Your Lagotto Romagnolo may get fat but doesn't grow and thrive.

If Your Lagotto Romagnolo gets diarrhea (even from high quality foods), check with your vet. There may be an ingredient in the food that doesn't interact well with Your Lagotto Romagnolo's digestive system. Ask the vet for a recommendation. If the next high quality food gets the same results, then Your Lagotto Romagnolo may have an internal illness or food allergy that the vet can diagnose.

What If You Don't Want to Crate Train?

You might think that crates are great for shipping cargo, but that dogs are living creatures who deserve better than that. To you, bringing a dog into your home is adding to your family.

It's not a toy to put in the crate while you're busy and take out a few hours when you have time. You believe that's not fair to the dog. Crate training may be a popular method for housetraining, but you don't have to do this to successfully train Your Lagotto Romagnolo.

As you're training the dog to wait between potty breaks or until you return home, you can isolate him in a smaller area.

A bathroom, laundry room or tiled kitchen is a good choice. The room needs to have an easy to clean floor.

Either close the door or add a baby gate. When you're at home, use the baby gate so that you can observe the dog and so that he doesn't feel punished by being away from you. You can also watch for the physical signs that he needs a potty break.

Dogs have their own signature moves - some seem agitated, restless or shake when they need to have a break. Others sniff in a circle and begin squatting when the time comes. You still need to follow the same approach for establishing a regular feeding schedule and follow-up with potty breaks.

When you come home to take the dog out to go potty, put the leash on him and head directly outside. Don't let him run around the house celebrating his freedom. In his excitement, he'll leave a puddle on the rug - not because he's mad at you, but because his enthusiasm overcame his bladder control.

Crate training advocates insist that this is the best and fastest way to housetrain a dog. Opponents totally disagree, countering that the difference of a few weeks is nothing compared to having a well-adjusted dog that feels like a member of the family rather than a prisoner of war most of the day.

If Your Lagotto Romagnolo is in a small room, he probably has far more space than in a crate. He also has a tall ceiling above him, so he feels free and happy. He can designate a spot in the room for an emergency potty and still have room to get away from it.

Your Lagotto Romagnolo is going to be a member of your family for many years. So what if it takes a little longer to house train him? You may have to use the small room training location for nights until he's old enough or well trained enough to wait until morning to go potty.

This isn't the time to weaken and put him in your bed. You'll both wake up in a chilly puddle. Give him time to adjust to the training, and then you can welcome him to a soft bed in your room, or surrender the extra pillow if you choose.

Epilogue

With that, we finished this little book. Now you have all the knowledge you need to help Your Lagotto Romagnolo, to improve its intellect and get its best behavior.

I won't say it's easy, but with work, commitment and constancy, I promise you the change will be clear, evident and huge... and what's best: the bond between you and your Lagotto Romagnolo would strengthen.

I tried to explain everything clearly, but if you have doubts, please, just ask. You can write to me to sencilloyrapido@gmail.com, and I will be glad to help.

Chin up, and good work!

Printed in Great Britain
by Amazon

29987604R00068